T0011089

WARMING PLANET

By Raymond Bergin

Consultant: David L. Fox
Professor of Earth & Environmental Sciences
University of Minnesota

BEARPORT
PUBLISHING

Minneapolis, Minnesota

Credits

Cover and title page, © Dragonvanish/iStockphoto, © sandsun/iStockphoto; 4–5, © Chris McLennan /Alamy; 6–7, © Walter Myers/Getty; 8–9, © VectorMine/iStockphoto; 10–11, © rmitsch/iStockphoto; 11, © Sara Winter/Shutterstock; 12, © captureandcompose/ Shutterstock; 12–13, © 3DSculptor/iStockphoto; 14–15, © leonello/iStockphoto; 16, © portokalis/iStockphoto; 17, © serkan mutan/Alamy; 18–19, © Moorefam/Getty; 20–21, © Nature Picture Library/Alamy; 22–23, © Daniiielc/iStockphoto; 24–25, © Daniel Grill/Getty; 26–27, © Audrius Venclova/Getty; 28, © georgeclerk/iStockphoto; 29, © VladimirFLoyd/iStockphoto, © Pheelings media/Shutterstock, © Tero Vesalainen/ Shutterstock, © Jacek Chabraszewski/Shutterstock, © Alexander Raths/Shutterstock.

President: Jen Jenson
Director of Product Development: Spencer Brinker
Senior Editor: Allison Juda
Associate Editor: Charly Haley
Senior Designer: Colin O'Dea

Library of Congress Cataloging-in-Publication Data

Names: Bergin, Raymond, 1968- author.
Title: Warming planet / by Raymond Bergin.
Description: Minneapolis, Minnesota : Bearport Publishing Company, [2022] |
  Series: What on earth? climate change explained | Includes
  bibliographical references and index.
Identifiers: LCCN 2021039164 (print) | LCCN 2021039165 (ebook) | ISBN
  9781636915609 (library binding) | ISBN 9781636915678 (paperback) | ISBN
  9781636915746 (ebook)
Subjects: LCSH: Global warming--Juvenile literature. | Climatic
  changes--Juvenile literature.
Classification: LCC QC981.8.G56 B4418 2022 (print) | LCC QC981.8.G56
  (ebook) | DDC 577.27/6--dc23
LC record available at https://lccn.loc.gov/2021039164
LC ebook record available at https://lccn.loc.gov/2021039165

Copyright © 2022 Bearport Publishing Company. All rights reserved. No part of this publication may be reproduced in whole or in part, stored in any retrieval system, or transmitted in any form or by any means, electronic, mechanical, photocopying, recording, or otherwise, without written permission from the publisher.

For more information, write to Bearport Publishing, 5357 Penn Avenue South, Minneapolis, MN 55419. Printed in the United States of America.

Contents

Melting Away

A hungry polar bear and her cubs swim toward a large chunk of ice floating in the Arctic Ocean. Once there, they set out to hunt for seals, which usually live on and around the **sea ice**. But they find none. The tired and hungry family is forced to swim to the next slab of ice. But they can't go on like this for much longer.

The sea ice polar bears use for traveling, hunting, and resting is melting away as the previously frozen Arctic warms up. What on Earth is happening?

Arctic ice is melting fast. And it isn't being replaced nearly as quickly as it once was. Recently, the region has been hotter during warm months and doesn't get as cold for as long during cooler parts of the year.

Temperature Swings

Throughout its history, Earth has gone through long stretches of hotter and colder temperatures. There have been at least five periods in the past when the planet got significantly colder for a long stretch of time. During these cooling periods, huge sheets of ice covered large parts of the globe. Earth's larger **ice ages** lasted tens to hundreds of millions of years. Then, the planet warmed back up.

The most recent ice age began 2.6 million years ago. It lasted until about 11,000 years ago.

Keeping the Heat

Our planet is warm enough for life because of something called the greenhouse effect. Trees, soil, and water **absorb** the sunlight that reaches Earth, which creates heat. At the same time, sunlight bounces off ice and other light-colored parts of the planet's surface.

But even during an ice age when the planet is covered in a lot of light-bouncing ice, our Earth holds on to heat. Certain gases around the planet, including **carbon dioxide**, naturally collect in the air and trap some of the heat from **reflected** light. We call these gases greenhouse gases because they act like the heat-trapping glass of a greenhouse.

Earth's average temperature is 60 degrees Fahrenheit (15.6 degrees Celsius). Without the natural greenhouse effect, our planet's average temperature would be -0.4°F (-18°C). Most of the life on Earth could not survive if it were that cold.

The sun's light comes to Earth. Its heat warms the planet.

Some of the reflected sunlight is trapped around Earth by greenhouse gases.

Sunlight that hits dark surfaces is absorbed as heat.

Sunlight that hits light surfaces bounces back into space.

9

Passing Gas

Greenhouse gases make Earth warm enough to live on. But humans are adding so many of these gases into the air that we have changed the natural pattern of Earth's heating and cooling.

We burn **fossil fuels** to power our cars, factories, and homes. But this process releases a lot of greenhouse gas, especially carbon dioxide, into the air. Adding more of these gases into our air traps more heat around Earth. As a result, air and ocean temperatures are rising. The planet is heating up, and the **climate**—or the usual weather in an area—is changing.

Methane is another greenhouse gas that is warming the planet. The burps, farts, and manure of farm animals add methane to the air.

Factories add a lot of greenhouse gases into our air.

Looking to the Past for Answers

Scientists study ancient ice and trees to learn about Earth's previous climates. The thickness of ice layers and tree rings tells them how much snow or rain fell in years past, what the temperatures were, and the amount of greenhouse gases that were in the air.

By studying this information, scientists have learned that when levels of greenhouse gases increase, temperatures rise and Earth's climate changes. They also know that today's warming is happening much faster than it did at the end of the last ice age.

The rings of trees can tell scientists about the climate long ago.

Today, scientists use satellites flying around Earth to keep track of global temperatures.

Average temperatures have risen 2.12°F (1.18°C) since the late 1800s. Scientists say they may rise as much as 9°F (5°C) by 2100.

Small Shifts, Huge Differences

The world is getting warmer a couple of degrees at a time. That may not sound like much. But small temperature shifts make a huge difference.

During the most recent ice age, Earth's average temperature was only about 11°F (6°C) colder than it is now. But it was still cool enough to cause ice to cover one-third of the planet! So much water turned to ice that oceans were 400 feet (122 m) lower than they are now. The air also became very dry, and half as much rain fell as compared with today. More heat is sure to change things drastically again.

Some animals that lived in the cold climate of the last ice age could not survive the warm-up at the end of it. Woolly mammoths, giant sloths, and saber-toothed cats all died off as temperatures rose.

Extreme Weather

Around the world, many drier places are getting drier. Today's rising temperatures are leading to more **heat waves** and **droughts**. This hot, dry weather is also causing wildfires that burn out of control.

At the same time, many wet places are getting wetter. In wetter places, warmer air draws more **moisture** out of soil, **vegetation**, lakes, and oceans. The damp air forms clouds, and the moisture falls back down to Earth as heavy rain. Downpours that cause flooding are becoming more and more common.

Global warming is making **hurricanes** more powerful. The warmer the air gets, the more water a hurricane's spinning clouds pull up into the storm and the heavier the rainfall becomes.

Extreme droughts
are drying up rivers
across the world.

Rising Waters

As the air warms, oceans are warming, too. And this can cause some major problems to the land along the water.

Warmer water takes up more space. So, as the oceans are heating up, they are expanding. This means they are reaching farther onto land. The rising **sea level** has led to flooding along coasts and has even covered whole islands under the waves. Many animals—and people—living on islands and in coastal areas are beginning to flee their homes for higher ground.

Rising temperatures are causing sea ice to melt, which adds more water to the oceans. Every year, 666 billion tons (604 billion t) of melting ice enters oceans.

Damaged Homes

But even living farther inland doesn't guarantee safety for many animals. Among the creatures hit hard by global climate change are the world's orangutans. Rising temperatures have created longer dry seasons in their native homes. As a result, the fruit trees the animals rely on for food are disappearing. When food is **scarce**, orangutans have fewer babies and their population shrinks. The hotter, drier weather also leads to wildfires that are causing even more damage to the forests where they live.

Dry conditions led to huge wildfires in Australia during the summer of 2019 and 2020. The fires killed as many as 10,000 koalas. These animals are now in danger of **extinction.**

Orangutans are native to the islands of Sumatra and Borneo in Asia.

Humans Feel the Heat

Humans are affected by climate change, too. Droughts, wildfires, flooding rains, and monster hurricanes can destroy crops, damage homes, and force people to move. During heat waves, people can get very sick and can even die if they don't get enough water or have a way to cool off. The smoke of wildfires can cause breathing problems for those close to the fires as well as those who live hundreds of miles away.

If carbon dioxide levels, temperatures, and damaging weather keep causing harm, our crops will be smaller and less **nutritious.** Some places are already struggling to grow enough healthy food.

Collecting Carbon

Global warming is a huge threat. But a lot of people around the world are working hard to stop temperatures from rising much further.

To remove carbon dioxide from the air, governments and environmental groups are planting more trees and other plants. Plants remove carbon from the air and replace it with clean air for us to breathe. Scientists are also experimenting with machines that can suck carbon dioxide out of the air and pump it safely underground.

> The record-breaking 2020 Atlantic hurricane season included 30 tropical storms and 7 major hurricanes. It was the fifth straight year with an above-normal hurricane season.

Staying High, Dry, and Cool

The planet has already warmed enough that we can't prevent some of the effects of climate change. But **engineers** and scientists are helping to protect life on Earth by helping us **adapt** to the change.

Engineers are working to prevent flooding by building structures that block floodwaters and by planting vegetation along coasts that soaks up extra water. Scientists are developing new kinds of crops that can grow even during droughts. What else can we do to adapt to the change?

Light-colored roofs reflect heat instead of absorbing it. Green roofs, or rooftop gardens, can also help cool off hot cities. They create shade and cool the buildings and air around them.

Battle Global Warming!

The biggest cause of global warming is the burning of heat-trapping fossil fuels. To battle global warming, the best thing you can do is cut back on the energy you use.

Save electricity by turning off lights when you leave a room. Use LED lightbulbs, which use much less energy than fluorescent bulbs.

Unplug power cords and chargers when you're done with them. Some can continue to use power even when they aren't being used but are plugged in.

Heating water takes a lot of energy. Take short showers and wash your clothes in cold water.

Instead of getting a car ride, walk or bike places whenever it is possible and safe.

Plant a garden or window box and join tree-planting projects around town. Trees and plants suck carbon dioxide from the air.

Glossary

absorb to take in or soak up

adapt to change over time to survive in an environment or habitat

carbon dioxide a gas given off when fossil fuels are burned

climate the typical weather in a place

droughts long periods of time with dry weather

engineers people who are trained to design and build things to solve problems

extinction when a type of animal or plant dies out

fossil fuels fuels such as coal, oil, and gas made from the remains of plants and animals that died millions of years ago

heat waves very hot weather that lasts for several days

hurricanes circular storms that form over the ocean with heavy rains and winds of at least 74 miles per hour (119 kph)

ice ages periods of time when massive sheets of ice covered large areas of Earth

moisture water contained in something such as a cloud

nutritious having substances that a person or animal needs to be healthy and grow properly

reflected bounced back

scarce hard to find

sea ice ice formed by the freezing of seawater

sea level the average height of the sea's surface

vegetation different types of plants, including grasses, bushes, and trees

Read More

McDaniel, Melissa. *Facing a Warming World (A True Book: Understanding Climate Change).* New York: Children's Press, 2020.

McGregor, Harriet. *Heat Wave Horror! (Uncharted: Stories of Survival).* Minneapolis: Bearport Publishing, 2021.

Minoglio, Andrea. *Our World Out of Balance: Understanding Climate Change and What We Can Do.* San Francisco: Blue Dot Kids Press, 2021.

Learn More Online

1. Go to **www.factsurfer.com** or scan the QR code below.

2. Enter "**Warming Planet**" into the search box.

3. Click on the cover of this book to see a list of websites.

Index

About the Author

Raymond Bergin is a writer living in New Jersey. When he was born 52 years ago, his hometown could expect 10 days a year above 90°F (32°C). Today, it can expect 15 of those very hot days. By the time he is 80, there could be more than 30 days a year above 90°F.